Written by
ANN HARTH

Illustrated by
DION HAMILL

A Harcourt Achieve Imprint

www.Steck-Vaughn.com
1-800-531-5015

Goodbye

Steck-Vaughn Take 3!
Originally published as Highlights! © 2005
Blake Publishing Pty Ltd, 108 Main Road,
Clayton South VIC 3168, Australia

Exclusive United States Distribution: Harcourt Achieve Inc.

Harcourt Achieve Inc.
10801 N. Mopac Exp., Bldg. 3
Austin, Texas 78759
www.HarcourtAchieve.com

ISBN-13: 978-1-4189-4492-6
ISBN-10:   1-4189-4492-0

© 2008 Harcourt Achieve Inc.

All rights reserved. No part of the material protected
by this copyright may be reproduced or utilized in any form
or by any means, in whole or in part, without permission
in writing from the copyright owner. Requests for
permission should be mailed to: Harcourt Achieve Inc.,
Paralegal Department, 6277 Sea Harbor Drive,
Orlando, FL 32887.

Steck-Vaughn is a trademark of Harcourt Achieve Inc.

Printed in China

1 2 3 4 5 6 7 8 788 14 13 12 11 10 09 08 07

Contents

1. Hot Days 4
2. Another Chance 12
3. Not Much Time 20
4. Nu Returns 26
5. The Rescue Fire 32
6. The Last Sign 40

1. Hot Days

A plane crash in the ocean has stranded Nalini and Zed on a small island. They hope that a rescue plane will find them and take them home. In the meantime, they sleep in a cave, drink fresh water from a stream, and eat fallen coconuts.

Each day, they use seaweed to make a sign on the beach to signal the rescue planes. But the planes have only flown over after high tide has washed the sign away. They have tried unsuccessfully to build a fire to signal the plane.

Then they meet Nu, the only other human inhabitant of the island. He has shown Nalini and Zed how to build a fire and find food.

Now Nalini and Zed always keep a fire burning on the rocks outside the cave. But the weather has been wet, making it difficult for them to find dry wood for the fire.

"If we had a lot of dry wood, we could make a huge fire. Then someone would find us," says Nalini.

Zed rolls over a wet log and says, "It takes days to dry wood in here."

Each day, Nalini and Zed keep the fire burning and make a "HELP" sign on the beach with seaweed. When the tide is low, they help Nu gather fruit and coconuts for the hurricane season.

As they sit by the fire with Nu, Nalini says to Zed, "We've been here for twenty days."

"Nu has been here for twenty years," Zed replies.

"I found it hard at first," Nu says, "but then I wanted to be alone."

Nalini gazes at him in amazement and says, "You want to stay on this island?"

"Yes, it's my home now," Nu says. Zed stops eating his berries and also stares at Nu in surprise.

Nu picks up Nalini's basket and tells her, "You weave good baskets now. You two could live on this island forever."

"But we want to go home," Nalini replies.

Nu stands up abruptly. "We need to collect more food. When the hurricanes begin, we may need to stay in the hill cave for days."

Nalini shudders when she imagines being cooped up in the small, dark cave up the hill, stranded by heavy rains. They need to be rescued before the hurricanes begin.

After the tide recedes the next day, Nu says, "Let's go swimming, and then we have to work."

"All right," Zed agrees, "but first we need to make the seaweed sign and build up the fire."

Nalini scampers back and forth with seaweed to finish the sign. Then she looks up at the cave, where Zed has built a large fire. Zed and Nu join Nalini on the beach.

"That's the biggest sign we've ever made," Zed says.

"And the biggest fire we've ever made, too," Nalini replies.

"Come on," Nu says. "I want to swim."

2. Another Chance

Enjoying the cool shade, Nalini, Zed, and Nu walk through the trees to the pool. Nalini sits in the soft emerald-green grass at the edge of the pool. Nu swims under the waterfall, and Zed floats on his stomach in the clear water.

Seeing Zed floating in the water makes Nalini sad. She remembers when she saw Zed floating in the ocean after the crash and feared that he was dead.

Nalini jumps into the pool, and she and Zed play in the water all morning while Nu sleeps in the sun. Nalini and Zed drink water and eat berries. The sun is high in the sky when they climb out to dry off.

"Ready to work?" Nu asks, rested and excited after his long morning nap. Knowing they have to help gather food, Nalini stifles a groan and forces herself to smile and nod.

Throwing a basket to Nalini and a basket to Zed, Nu says, "Let's get going."

They follow Nu along a path through the forest to a thicket of passion fruit vines. After filling their baskets, they sit in the shade and munch on the sweet, ripe, juicy fruit. "When we're rescued, you can come with us, Nu," Nalini says.

Nu shakes his head and says, "No, I want to remain here."

"But aren't you lonely here?" asks Zed.

"No, I have become accustomed to living alone. Besides, you're here now," Nu says.

Nalini and Zed glance at each other, eyebrows raised. "Nu," says Nalini, "don't you want us to leave?"

"No, I don't," Nu replies, looking at his feet.

"But Nalini and I want to go home," says Zed.

"But if you're rescued, someone might find out about me and insist that I return to the mainland," Nu says.

"We won't tell anyone," Zed promises.

Carrying their fruit-filled baskets, Zed and Nalini climb up to the small hill cave. They squeeze through the small entrance into the dark, dank cave. "I don't want to stay in here," Nalini grumbles.

"I don't either," says Zed, "but we might have to."

Zed empties their baskets onto a mat made from palm leaves, next to a large pile of coconuts. "Let's fill the baskets once more and then go back to the pool," he says. "I'll race you!"

Nalini dashes off through the trees with Zed close behind her. When they reach the passion fruit vines, they stop to rest and notice that Nu is gone. Suddenly, Nalini looks up and says, "Zed, listen!"

As Zed tilts his head, his eyes light up, and he grins. "The plane is back, " he shouts gleefully.

"They'll see the sign and the fire," Nalini shouts. "We're going to be rescued!"

Zed and Nalini sprint toward the beach.

"What is the first thing you'll do when we get back home?" Zed calls.

"I'm going to read six books," Nalini shouts back. "What will you do?"

"I'm going to eat Mom's homemade ice cream," Zed laughs.

As they approach the beach, Nalini looks into the sky, expecting to see the plane circling nearby. Instead, she sees a speck retreating into the distance and hears the soft sound of the plane flying away. "Zed," she whispers, "it's gone."

"Maybe they've gone to get help," Zed says, puzzled. "They must have seen the fire and our sign."

Nalini runs down to the beach, looking for the fire, but she doesn't see anything. "Oh, no, Zed, the fire has gone out, and the seaweed sign is gone, too!" Nalini feels like she might begin to cry.

3. Not Much Time

"Zed, we should have been here! We should never have left the fire," Nalini wails. Zed doesn't say anything, but he pats Nalini's back before he walks away.

Nalini sinks down with her head on her knees, wondering if another plane will come before the hurricane season starts. The sun beats down from the sky, and heat radiates up from the sand, drying out Nalini's throat. Nalini knows she needs water, but she doesn't care. Giving up, she only wants to sleep and never have to wake up. She collapses on the sand and lies there until the sea reaches her toes and thunder rumbles across the sky.

Then Nalini slowly sits up, her head pounding. She crawls to the rocks and shakily climbs to the cave as raindrops begin to fall.

Inside the cave, Nalini curls in a ball on the floor and sleeps.

"Nalini, Nalini, wake up, " Zed pleads, his voice full of fear. "Drink this, Nalini," Zed says urgently, as he drips water into her mouth.

"Zed?" Nalini's voice sounds like a croaking frog.

"Shh, don't try to talk. Just drink some more."

Nalini swallows and swallows. "My head hurts," she moans.

Zed says, "You were in the sun too long."

"The plane," Nalini says, "we missed the plane."

"We will try again tomorrow," Zed says gently.

Nalini listens to the rain fall heavily on the ledge outside the cave. Is the hurricane season beginning? Suddenly she feels very scared, thinking she will go crazy in that small, dark cave on the hill.

When morning comes, the rain has stopped. Nalini takes a long drink of water and walks out of the cave. "How are you feeling today?" Zed asks, as he tries to start a fire.

"I'm all right," Nalini replies, sitting down next to him and looking out across the water.

"Nalini," Zed says, "this is our last chance. We have to be persistent, and we can't afford to get discouraged." Nalini looks up at the heavy rain clouds.

"We have to make the 'HELP' sign again and again and keep the fire burning," Zed says.

"Yes, we can take turns. I know we can't leave anything to chance," Nalini nods. "I'll bring more dry seaweed and wood from the cave, and I'll gather some fresh wood to dry inside."

"We have enough dry wood to keep the fire going for a few days," Zed says. "We will be saved when the rescue plane comes again."

Nalini looks at her brother and says, "We'll be saved if the rescue plane comes again."

4. Nu Returns

Zed counts the twenty-six lines on the cave floor, one for each day they've been on the island since the crash. Nalini and Zed haven't seen Nu in a couple of days, not since he said he wanted them to stay. Why is Nu hiding from them?

Nalini and Zed prepare for a rescue plane to arrive and for the hurricane season to start. They make a huge, seaweed "HELP" sign as soon as hide tide recedes each day. They keep the fire burning on the ledge throughout the day, and they light the fire inside the cave at night. They take turns staying awake to keep the fire burning. They gather coconuts and fruit each day to store in the small cave on the hill. In the meantime, heavy, nightly rains leave puddles inside the entrance of the big cave.

Every night, Nalini dreams that she can see her mother's face and feel her mother's hands stroking her head.

Early one morning, as Nalini sits by the fire in the dark cave, she remembers their first days on the island. At first, the island was their sanctuary. Then, the sunshine and the beauty of the island made their experience seem like an adventure. But the longer they have to stay on the island, the less it seems like an adventure. Now she is afraid they will be stranded on the island forever.

Nalini leans her head against the cave wall. Suddenly, a ray of sunshine streams into the cave and touches Nalini's face. As the sun warms Nalini, she starts to feel better. She jumps up quickly, lights the fire outside the cave, and climbs down to make another sign on the beach.

When she has finished the sign, she writes her name in the sand with her finger. Then she sits quietly for a long time, until she feels someone touch her shoulder.

Startled, Nalini jumps up and spins around, exclaiming, "Nu! Where have you been?"

"I needed to think," Nu says simply.

"You're back, Nu!" Zed calls, running toward them across the sand.

Nu speaks quietly, saying, "I realized that I was being selfish, and I am ready to help you. Before, I didn't want rescuers to find you because I feared that they might force me to leave this island. I have enjoyed your company, too." He sits down in the sand. "But you belong with your family, and I can't continue to keep you away from them. Now I know I am ready to help you return home."

"How can you help us?" Zed asks eagerly.

"I think that the plane will return today because the sun is shining," Nu says. "You still have one more chance, but we'll need a big fire."

5. The Rescue Fire

"A big fire?" Nalini asks Nu.

"Yes, we need a huge fire, right here," Nu says as he scrapes a circle in the dry sand.

"But we don't have enough dry wood to keep a huge fire going," Zed says, frowning. "We need more dry wood."

"I'll show you where we can get dry wood," Nu says, walking into the trees and turning toward the cave.

"OK, let's go," Nalini says hopefully. Mud squeezes up between Nalini's toes as she follows Nu into the rainforest.

"How will he find dry wood here in the wet rainforest?" Zed whispers to Nalini. They continue through the forest until they reach the back of the hurricane season cave.

Just past the cave, Nu stops, points to the rock wall, and asks, "Do you think this is enough?" Dry branches, logs, and sticks—enough for twenty big fires—fill a hole in the rock wall. Nalini picks up a log and smiles, exclaiming, "It's dry!"

For the rest of the morning, Nalini, Zed, and Nu pile branches and logs in a large mound on the beach. Although the seaweed sign has washed away, they won't need it. The fire will be taller than Zed.

"Let's light the big fire from the small one on the ledge," Zed says as he puts one last branch on the pile.

Nalini and Zed follow Nu to the fire on the ledge. Nu climbs the rocks up to the ledge while Nalini and Zed wait on the sand. Suddenly, Nalini hears a buzzing noise high in the sky. "I hear an airplane approaching. We must light the fire quickly, Nu!" she exclaims.

Nu looks down at Nalini and Zed and then up at the plane. He quickly grabs a burning stick, jumps to the sand, and races toward the huge pile of wood. Zed and Nalini sprint after him.

The plane buzzes in a circle over the sea, and then flies farther away. Nu stops next to the pile of wood, looks up at the plane, and then looks directly at Nalini and Zed.

37

"Please don't tell them about me," Nu says, as he pushes the burning stick into the pile of seaweed and wood. Then he turns and disappears into the rainforest.

The seaweed and wood ignite, and flames leap into the sky. Smoke billows upward, stinging Nalini's eyes.

As Nalini runs down the beach away from the smoke, she looks into the sky but sees nothing. She no longer hears the buzzing of the plane. Is it already gone, taking their last chance to be rescued with it?

Zed runs up beside her. "Look!" he shouts, pointing to the flames shooting up over their heads.

"The plane is gone, Zed," Nalini says sadly.

"It can't be gone. The pilot must have seen the fire."

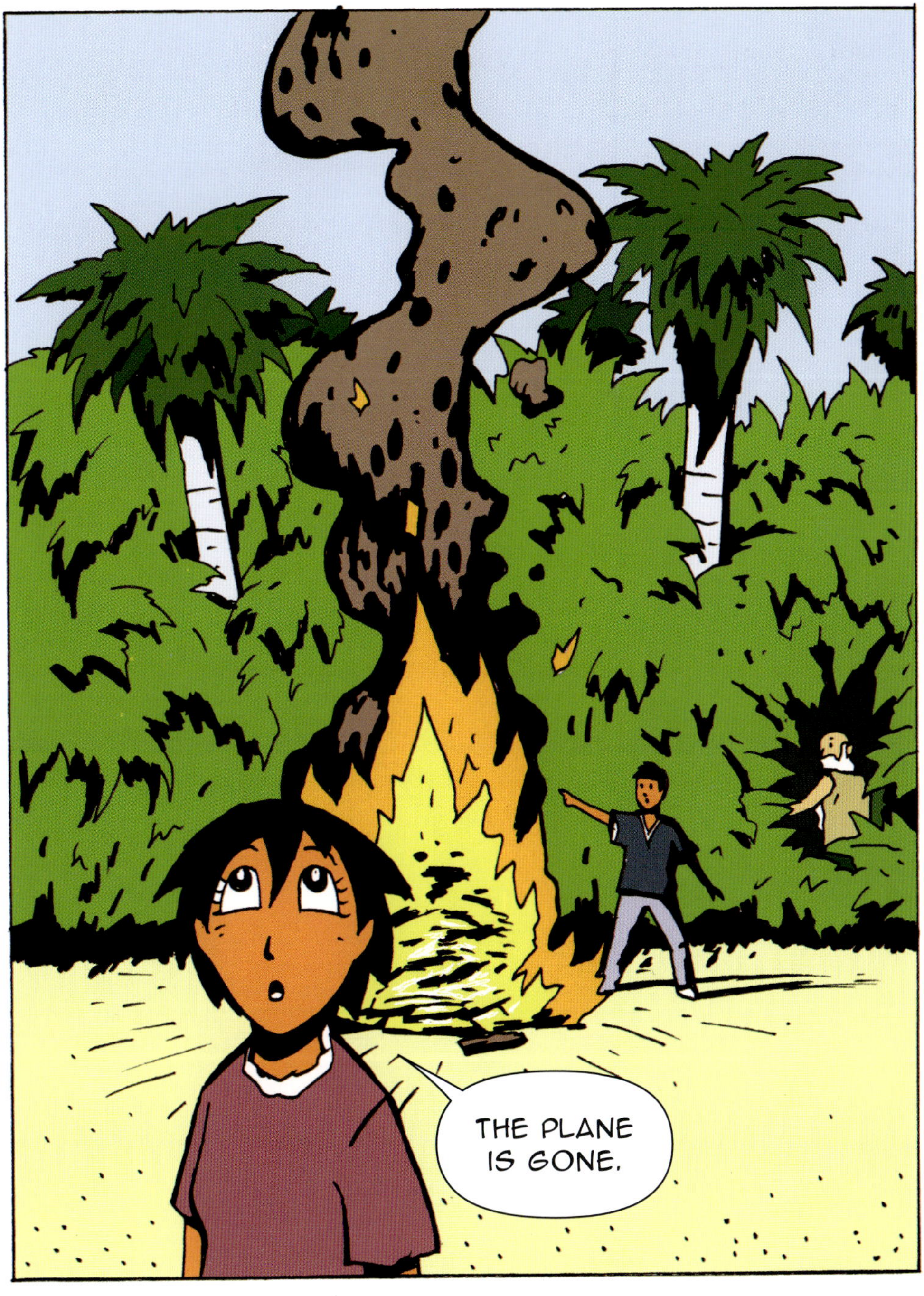
THE PLANE IS GONE.

6. The Last Sign

"Wait, Nalini, listen," says Zed excitedly. Nalini looks up. What is that loud sound coming from behind the mountain? Nalini and Zed spin around and see the plane fly low over their heads.

"Here!" Nalini and Zed scream, jumping up and down. "We're here!"

As the plane banks to turn, it comes so close that Nalini can see a face in the window. She waves frantically and continues shouting, "Hello, hello! We're here!" The plane dips its wings and flies away, but Nalini and Zed know it will be back.

That night, Nalini and Zed sit outside the cave and look at the moonbeams reflecting on the water. "Tomorrow night we'll be home," Nalini sighs happily. "Do you think they will send a boat?" she asks.

"They might," Zed replies.

WE'RE HERE!

WE'RE HERE!

TOMORROW NIGHT WE'LL BE HOME.

"Hey, Zed, do you think we'll see Nu again?" Nalini asks after a moment of silence.

"No, I doubt it," says Zed.

"I wish we could thank him for everything. Do you think he'll be all right?" Nalini asks.

"Yes, he'll be all right," Zed says, "because this is his home."

Just after sunrise the next morning, Nalini and Zed hear a helicopter approaching the island. They see it flying back and forth, looking for a place to land.

Nalini glances toward the rainforest, hoping to see Nu again to say goodbye and to thank him for his help. But then the helicopter hovers and lands, and the pilot hops out, smiling at them. "Do you kids need a ride home?" he asks.

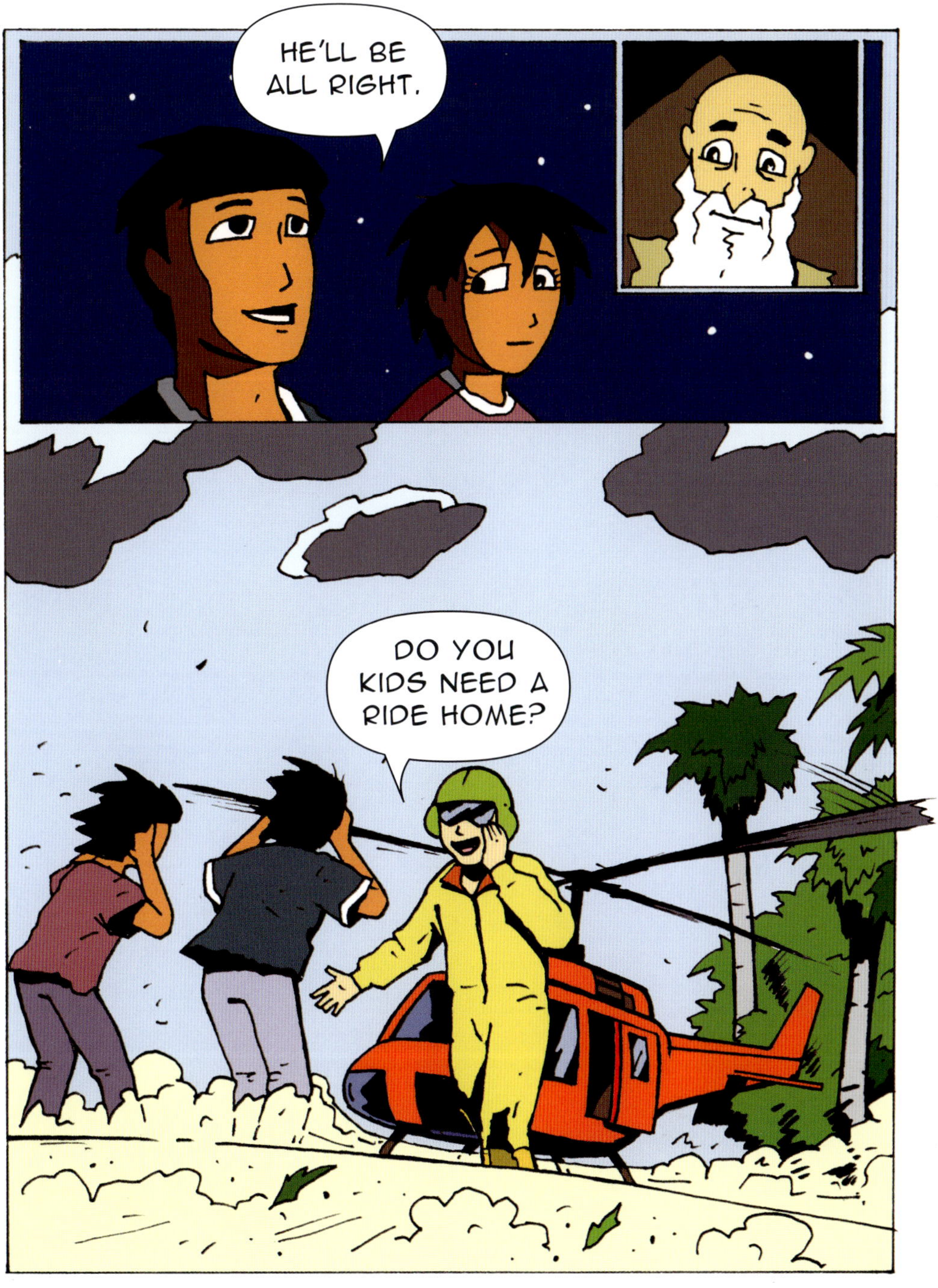
HE'LL BE ALL RIGHT.
DO YOU KIDS NEED A RIDE HOME?

Nalini and Zed laugh and climb into the helicopter. Zed holds Nalini's hand as the helicopter lifts into the air and the first drops of rain hit the helicopter's windows.

"We'll have to fly straight over the top of the island to miss the bad weather," the helicopter pilot tells them.

Zed and Nalini look out the window at their island. They see their rock, the opening to the cave, and the shiny line of their stream. Nalini sighs, thinking of Nu spending the hurricane season alone in his small cave.

45

As the helicopter flies to the other side of the island, the pilot looks out the window at the beach. "When did you kids make that sign? It wasn't there yesterday," he says.

"What sign?" Zed asks.

Nalini looks out of the window and sees a huge seaweed sign across the beach that says "Goodbye."

"Remember, Zed?" Nalini says, squeezing his hand.

"Oh, yes," Zed replies, winking at Nalini. "We made a different sign every day," he says. "We were very good at it."

Nalini smiles and looks at the island one last time. "Goodbye, Nu," she whispers.

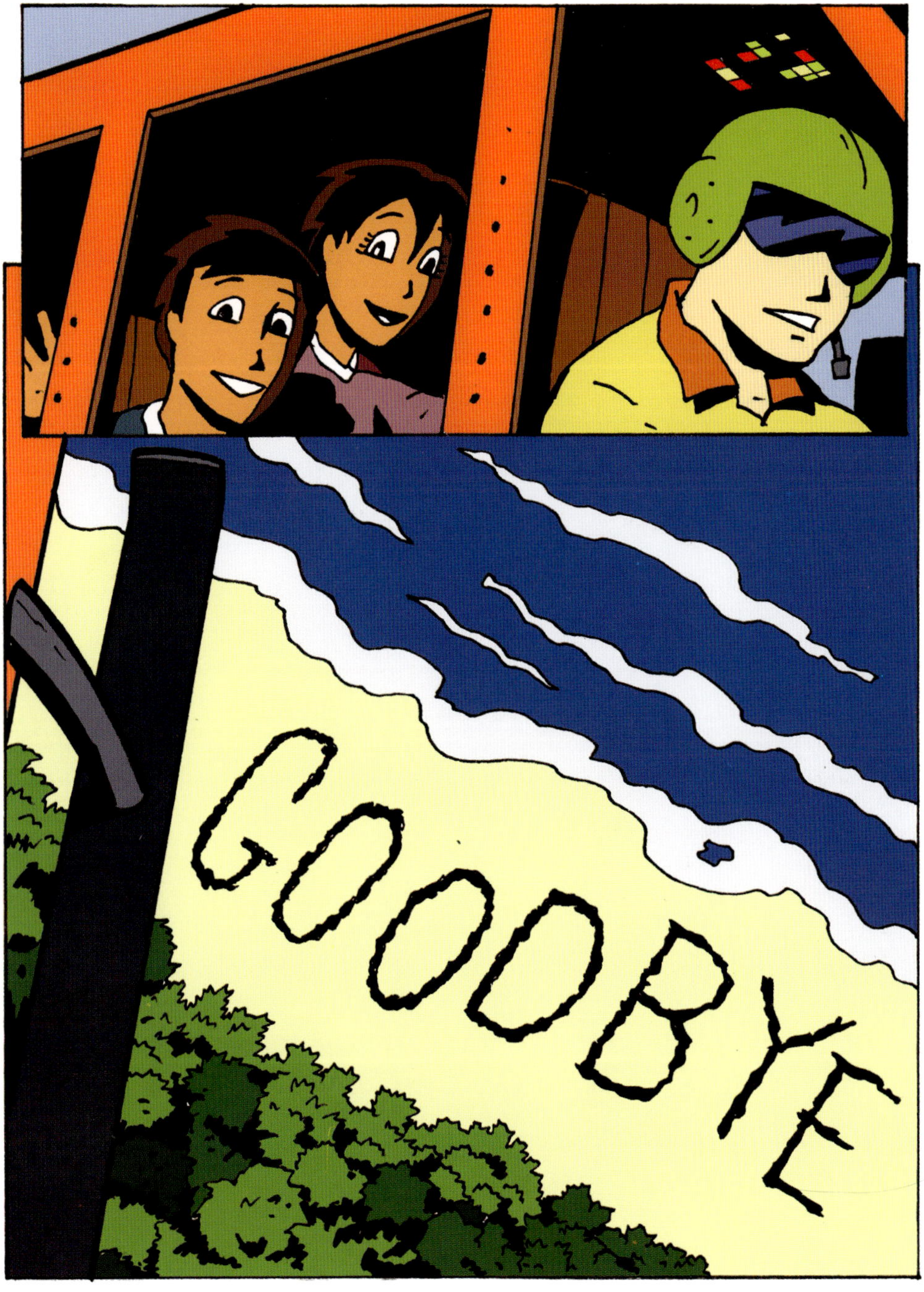
GOODBYE

Glossary

collapses *(verb)* falls down

gazes *(verb)* looks at for a long time

ignite *(verb)* catch on fire

inhabitant *(noun)* someone who lives in a particular place

persistent *(adjective)* continuing without giving up

radiates *(verb)* gives off; sends out

sanctuary *(noun)* a safe and protected place

stifles *(verb)* holds back; smothers

stranded *(verb)* left stuck in a bad place

urgently *(adverb)* in a way needing immediate attention